The Magnificent Seven

Seven Swords to Slay Your Dragons

Volume I

In Him,

Mark Burlingame

Rev. Mark Burlingame

Rev. Mark Burlingame has been in the ministry for over thirty years. He is available for teaching, preaching and coaching to prepare Spirit-filled believers to complete the Great Commission.

You can reach him at markalisa@gmail.com or mark@newbeginnings.org

The Magnificent Seven
Seven Swords to Slay Your Dragons: Volume I
by Rev. Mark Burlingame

© 2016 by Rev. Mark Burlingame

ISBN-13: 978-1533497512
ISBN-10: 1533497516

Printed in the United States of America

Contents

The Magnificent Seven

Introduction

I have been a student of the Bible since 1980. For the first two of those years I was an unsaved seeker. But for the last thirty years, although a believer in Christ, I am still a seeker. I have used the Bible to gain knowledge of the Holy One, to gain inspiration for preaching, and to gain information for teaching others about the way of faith. The Bible has been for me an anchor to hold on to when the storms of life were trying to pull me down to the abyss.

I have found that as I am growing older, I have a strong desire to leave something behind as a legacy -- something that will encourage other seekers who are coming along behind me after I am gone. So I have stated in my will that my nephew Bobby will inherit my gun collection. I have also given away various things in the past several years, among them my ample book collection which had filled up three walls and of which I was very proud. After all, I had spent a lifetime gathering them. But one day the Spirit challenged my heart to consider what benefit those books were bringing to anyone when they just stayed on those dusty shelves. Reluctantly, I agreed with Him. Over the next six months, I gave away almost one hundred books to individuals and various churches.

But I believe that this book you are holding, The Magnificent Seven, is the best gift I have given, and that it will bless those who decide to ponder its pages.

Throughout the years of my walk with the Lord, the seven verses expounded herein have guided, encouraged and even rebuked me more times than I would like to admit. I pray that as you meditate on these timely truths, they will serve to bring you closer to the God who reveals Himself in the Holy Scriptures for all to see.

The following Magnificent Seven Scriptures have influenced my life.

In Him,
Rev. M.A. Burlingame

Scripture 1

*But without faith it is impossible to please Him,
for he who comes to God must believe that
He is, and that He is a rewarder of those
who diligently seek Him.*

Hebrews 11:6

From the snake handlers to the shouting,
sweat-covered evangelists, through my whole
Christian life I have heard about the need for
faith! Do you want to know something? Those
who preach the faith message are absolutely,
positively correct. Even though their methods
could be wrong (rattlesnakes don't like being
held and kissed, and even though God is an-
cient He is not hard of hearing), their message
is right on.

The truth of the matter is that there are
two major enemies of our faith. The evil twins
of doubt and fear have plagued the children of
God since the beginning of time. Doubt was in
the garden when Adam and Eve took that first
horrible bite. Fear was rising up like a tsunami

when the spies saw how big their enemies were on the other side of the river. The consequences of succumbing to that fear cost them another lap in the desert that extended to forty years.

There are two words in this verse from Hebrews that have challenged me, encouraged me and kept the evil twins of doubt and fear at bay these past thirty years. (By the way, despite my age, I still run a mile a day and do pushups, at least on most days). Back to the main point, the two words I am referring to are faith and reward.

I believe without a shadow of doubt that my faith will determine my reward. That might sound like a theology of faith by works to the 'sloppy agape' crowd, but we should remember that Paul encouraged his readers with the words run for the prize. That gives the picture of diligent effort, not of an easy ride through a luxurious life. By the way, when did it become work to diligently seek the Lord? Maybe the reason we are not as blessed as we want to be is because we are seeking the wrong things. We are called to seek Christ Himself. As the Word of God states, all blessings flow from God out of our relationship with Him!

We are also challenged by the word diligently at the end of this verse. Diligence is defined as showing perseverance and application in whatever is undertaken. It is also described as pursuing something, or as in our case someone, with painstaking effort. Perhaps it is our love and relationship to Him that opens the door to receiving rewards from Him. Out of that love, every good deed from helping a neighbor move to baking them a pie is an act of faith and will be rewarded.

One precious lady in our Bible study diligently brings delicious pies, cakes and cobblers to our gathering on Monday nights. No one asked her or assigned her to do it, but hers is an act of love that brings joy to all of us. I would like to think that it is my anointed teaching that has brought faithful members to the Bible study for the last ten years -- but I must admit the truth. It is not my teaching that draws them, it is Fran's wonderful pies. The joy of the Lord in her life that obviously bubbles out is evidence of God's reward to her. Her message does not come out in fiery sermons but rather from a loving, serving, joyful life.

When I am bombarded with dark, negative thoughts about ministry and life (that everyone experiences but that no one admits to, for fear of losing face), the Holy Spirit gently reminds me that tomorrow is another day. It is okay to just go to bed early. Tomorrow will be better, my faith will be stronger, and my rewards will be worth the tears and the fears. Tomorrow will provide another chance to run for the prize: Him.

Scripture 2

Jesus said to him, I am the way, the truth, and the life. No one comes to the Father except through Me.

John 14:6

This verse from the Gospel of John is one of my favorite Scriptures. Through it, the Spirit has given me revelation with which to battle cults and false doctrine. But this verse also makes Christianity the most prejudice religion in the entire world! Yes, it says that Jesus is the way, the only way, to God. There are not many paths to enlightenment -- just one -- and sometimes it is a narrow one at that.

The world system would love to see a worldwide religion, a single currency, a one-world government, all of which would supposedly help mankind live in peace and tranquility. But in reality, these systems would pave the way for the coming anti-christ. This Scripture stands as a flaming and firm reminder that God the Father wants us all to join Him in heaven, and Jesus is the way through which we can do that. The entrance is only through a bloody cross that leads to a promised paradise; all other roads lead to hell not heaven.

It does not seem fair, does it? It is also not fair that God had to send his own Son to take on our stinking, festering sins in order for us to even have a chance of going to heaven. God is definitely not fair. But how soon do we forget that He is sovereign? Our beliefs may not be politically correct, but the fact remains that it is still "His way or the highway."

Many churches today are trying to be relevant by removing crosses from the church signs and sanctuaries. They do not want to offend new seekers. The problem is, if we take the cross and what it represents out of church, all we are left with is another social club.

I speak from experience. When I was about twenty-four years of age, I was growing marijuana with a friend and dealing in crystal meth on the side. I had a house, money, a beautiful wife and a pickup truck. I lived in rural Pennsylvania, by the way, where a pickup was standard equipment for a young man. I was definitely living the American dream (did I mention that I owned a pickup truck)? However, I must confess that inside my heart, something was seriously missing. The thought that kept running through my foggy mind was, There must be something more!

Have you been in that place? It is called the if-I-had-this disease. Because my life was empty, I thought that another gadget or possession must be missing, and that if I had that particular thing, I would find satisfaction. I was wrong. It is very frightening to have all the material possessions, and yet have no peace.

After seeking truth and peace in all the wrong places, and seek I did, all the way from Carlos Castraneda and his writings on Indian Spiritualism to Buddhism and Scientology, I finally grew desperate enough to pick up the Bible. Going from the fear of the book of Revelation to the truth of Proverbs finally brought me to the gospels of Jesus Christ and the road to salvation. The truth of the gospel led me to the way of the cross, and I have been living in Christ for over thirty-five years. Guess what. The path is narrow and Christ is the only way, the only truth and the only life. As far as I am concerned, we should put to rest any further arguments about the many paths to God! It does not help at all to argue with people about how to get to God. All we need to do is show them this Scripture and wish them a nice day! From there, our job is done and the Holy Spirit will take over.

Scripture 3

He has shown you, Oh man, what is good;
and what does the Lord require of you?
But to do justly, to love mercy and to walk
humbly with your Lord.

Micah 6:8

One of the main questions I have received from inquiring seekers of truth is the typical one of How can I know the will of God for my life? I guess that is an honest question and one that we really do not have the answer to when we begin a journey with the Lord.

I must confess that as I was growing up, I had no idea what my place in this world would be. Some people do seem to know their destiny. My friend Rick, for example, was certain from the time we were in junior high that he wanted to be a doctor. He took courses that would prepare him for medical school, and incidentally has been my doctor for the last thirty years. Rick even showed me how to put in upper backs, a 'ministry' that I still practice today on any willing victims that pass my way and are desperate enough to accept my offer.

I would have to admit, being immersed in the fantasy of the drug life of the '60s and '70s could have delayed my hearing the call from the Lord to the ministry by a year or even ten. I am referring to my ministry call, not my pseudo-medical call.

Back to the question, how can I know God's will for my life? Unless an angel drops a ladder on your head with a message from God himself, we really cannot know the future that God has for us. For most of us, God's will is worked out and walked out over a lifetime. Yes, God has made his plans very clear for a select few, but I think most of us more or less wander into it through the circumstances, storms and relationships we forge in our search for truth and purpose. Our Father did say that He would give us the desires of our hearts. It is very possible that the will of God is already planted within you and what you need to do is simply follow your heart!

With that being said, my discovery of this prophecy from Micah has definitely made the journey manageable and simpler. The requirements of the prophet are spelled out so clearly that even a new lamb starting his or her journey could greatly benefit from their simplicity and wisdom. I want to share what I gleaned from this verse with the hope that as these few points get you started, the Holy Spirit will take you the rest of the way.

- Do Justly. Do the right thing when no one is looking.

- Love Mercy. Choose to see the good in your brothers and sisters. It is definitely there if you look hard enough.

- Walk Humbly. We deserve nothing, but our loving Father holds nothing back.

It is the simple things in life that keep us in the end. Maybe we can't move mountains with our frail faith, but we can do what is right -- today.

Scripture 4

But seek first the kingdom of God and his
Righteousness, and all these things
will be added to you.

Matthew 6:33

Matthew was a tax collector before he was
a God-chaser. Coming from a place of wealth
to praying in a fish for supper must have left
him wondering sometimes about the choice he
made to leave his job and follow Jesus.

In order to answer God's call, Lisa and I
left a house with twenty acres of land and two
good jobs. She worked in the post office and
walked to work and I had ten years of experience as an equipment operator for the state
government. I must confess that from time
to time a contention arises between us when
things are not going well in our household
finance department. Don't you hate visiting
woulda-coulda-shoulda land?

I look back at the decision I made to take
my wife from a cozy country setting to the

projects of Baltimore city. Did I mention that she was shot during our second week there? I will save that story for another day. As one who teaches that a man should be the priest, provider and protector of his house, I have wrestled with the python of condemnation in that area from time to time. I think it is something over which we as men judge ourselves, often feeling that we have missed the mark. We could feel guilty on different fronts. Perhaps we are good priests but poor providers, or perhaps we are good providers but lacking in the spiritual skills to properly lead our families. Whichever the case, we feel condemned.

Our ministry of thirty years has been one of repairing the breeches, whereby we have gone into broken churches or new church plants and raised them up. People have told me that I have an apostolic ministry -- but titles don't pay bills. If you are in the ministry, you will understand what price we pay. It is called a life of walking by faith. This Scripture about putting the kingdom first is for those of you who have not yet built mega-churches or written best-selling books.

I have often encouraged myself over the years that I have made the kingdom of God first in my life and God will not forget my labors. I have also preached the same message to anyone else who is willing to listen. Even though I might be an old prophet with a bad back and a leaky bank account, I make no excuses for the passionate love for God that I have nurtured over the years. I have carried a passion for God that has burned in my heart sometimes to the point of madness in my quest to make and keep Jesus in first place. I plead guilty to the charge that I am addicted to the Spirit of the Living God. I have been frustrated, however, by feeling that the same is not true of the church. How can we settle for anything less then a day by day revelation of the Fathers' love, the Son's redemption and the Spirit's gentle touch?

Please do not misunderstand me. I like having stuff just as much as any of us. But we simply cannot compare what the world offers and what we experience in kingdom life. After all it does not say we cannot have stuff -- it just says "seek him first." Everything else will still be added.

I made my choice early in life to seek God above and before all else. Looking back over the years, I can testify that I have been richly blessed. I have traveled on ministry trips to

South America, Cuba, Haiti and two countries in Africa. I have met some of the most amazing people. My only regret is that I did not surrender sooner. Yes, my wife and I have counted the cost of ministry at times, but putting His kingdom first has assured us of front row seats to our eagerly awaited inheritance in our eternal home. Have you reserved your seats yet?

Scripture 5

But if the Spirit of Him who raised Jesus from the dead dwells in you, He who raised Christ from the dead will also give life to your mortal bodies through his Spirit who dwells in you.

Romans 8:11

I discovered this verse later in my journey. This verse is a present-day reminder of our ever-present source of power that allows us to live a life that is just plain impossible to live in our own strength.

The same death-defeating power that raised a dead man from the grave is available to us here on earth. And even more amazing, we do not have to die to get it! We can live like Jesus lived and function like Jesus functioned. If that same Spirit is living in me, why can't He work through me to do things I humanly cannot do? This verse gives me a supernatural promise in which to walk for the rest of my life..

This Scripture also gives me the faith to pray for healing for the sick, to cast out demons and to preach a supernatural message to a lost and dying people. It gives me the assurance that God can give any person, no matter how hopeless, a total makeover. Remember, God does not make bad people good; He makes dead people live! This supernatural life that He promised is for the here and now, not just the hereafter.

I cannot tell you in one chapter how many times this promise has come true in my life. One time, we were travelling back home from Lancaster, Pennsylvania after I had given my testimony there. We hit a horrible snowstorm. It was a wet, slippery snow. In the last part of the trip, we slid into a sharp corner and I lost control of the car. We went spinning broadside into the path of another car that was coming downhill opposite us. As I fought the wheel to gain control, the steering wheel was literally ripped out of my hand. And by nothing but divine intervention, in two quick turns of the wheel we were back in our lane and the oncoming car passed us, missing us by inches. Could it be that angels and the Holy Spirit are watching over us more then we realize?

On another occasion back in the '80s, when we were attending Elim Bible Institute, I travelled to North Carolina to complete my ministry requirements for my junior year. We hit a violent rainstorm out on an old country road, and we were hopelessly lost. I am sure you can relate to the predicament of being lost on a strange highway. We began to pray in earnest, which is easy to do when you are terrified, and the power of God began to fill that car. The overwhelming sense of peace hit us until it seemed we were just having a ride through the countryside on a sunny day. Nothing physically had changed. We were still driving on an old country road that we had never been on before in our lives, and it was still raining hard with bands of fog everywhere. What had changed was that God heard our desperate prayers and his Spirit quickened our mortal bodies. We knew it because of the manifest presence that assured us He was with us and was protecting us.

I believe that if you are a Christian, you are invincible until your destiny here on earth is completed. By the way, handling serpents and other foolish stunts are not in the invincible clause. Then, Father will take you home to meet the rest of the family, unless of course you prefer to handle things yourself. Good luck with that one!

Scripture 6

Blessed be the God and Father of our Lord Jesus Christ who has blessed us with every spiritual blessing in the heavenly places in Christ.

Ephesians 1:3

This Scripture is the one on which I base the most important truth that I teach: The Blessing Road. In a nutshell, God has already blessed us with every, that is every, spiritual blessing. The catch is that the spiritual blessings are in the heavenly places and we can only access them by being in Christ. In order to get blessings we must be born again and have faith that as we walk into these heavenly places, God releases gifts that will equip us for the journey home. By the way, the bumps in the road are intended to be stepping stones that will take us to higher heavenly places.

There is one more catch. The path that leads to the heavenly places can only be accessed through obedience. Sin does not take you towards the blessings. On the contrary, it drives you in the opposite direction down into what I sometimes refer to as 'vomit valley.' I know that statement garners a lot of resistance from those who preach a sloppy appropriation of love and grace. But the simple truth is that God's love is forever and it does not have any hooks as Bob Mumford states in his book The Agape Road. However, the blessing of the Lord only comes when we obey. God cannot and will not bless sin. He forgives sin, but that does not give us the license to misuse His abundant grace and excuse sin.

There is a remedy for sin. It is called repentance. Repentance requires a change of mind and a change of action. When we truly repent, we are instantly restored to the road of blessings. I hate to disappoint you, but insincere tears and merely saying the words "I'm sorry" do not count without true repentance -- without a change of mind and a change of heart.

God has never and will never stop loving us through our encounters with sin, but we are the ones who willingly walk away on a sinful trail of our own making. I do believe in eternal security. But I also believe that all actions have consequences, both good and bad. A good father will spank his child when that discipline is needed. God is no different.

Ten years ago I made some bad choices and I almost lost everything. I eventually repented, but it took me many years before the damage of my wrong choices was fully healed in my life. Certainly God loved me through it and lovingly restored me, yet it was one of the hardest times of my life. I had to pray diligently in order to constantly resist thoughts of failure and suicide that bombarded my mind. This went on for a full year after I had repented. Sin and self condemnation are pits that are easy to fall in to, but hard to climb out of.

I am sharing this as a man who has seen both sides of this truth: the blessings as well as the consequences. The scars of sin heal, but they heal painfully and slowly. If you have ever experienced the abasement of a dog eating its own vomit, maybe you can imagine how God feels when we choose to sin even though we know better. Yeech! Remember, grace is the supernatural ability to lead a Christ-like life not an excuse to sin as you please.

Stay in Christ, stay on the Blessing Road and keep walking in obedience. As you do, you

will enjoy the blessings here on earth and be-
yond this earth that your Father has in store for
you!

Scripture 7

*And they overcame him by the Blood of the
Lamb and by the Word of their testimony,
and they did not love their lives to the Death.*

Revelation 12:11

    I came to know Jesus thirty-three years ago
on January 3, 1982, at 12:30 p.m. at the Troy
Baptist Church. A young pastor named Garry
Zuber led me through the Four Spiritual Laws. I
had been searching for God for over two years
and could not seem to find Him anywhere. Pastor Garry gently explained to me that the God
I was seeking was to be found by a simple act
of my will and repentance toward God. I guess
I had been expecting to see angels or wanting
to see lightning strike or desiring some other
strange experience. But when I bowed my head
and said a simple prayer in sincerity of heart,
the light finally came on.

    I did not see angels, but I literally felt the
weight of my sins slowly lift away. The best way
to describe the experience was that I felt clean

again. I was very sure, even though I do not know why, but I was very certain that I would never be the same again. I knew that I would never again be alone, unloved or uncertain about the future in this world and the one to come.

Your testimony is your spiritual DNA. It becomes a part of you and something that no human being on earth can ever take away from you. You can lose your possessions, you can lose your health, you can lose friends and family -- but no one can take your encounter with God away from you. Your personal testimony is your best weapon to fight the battle against the world, the flesh and the devil! The cleansing of the blood of Christ, coupled with the declaration of your freedom, is more then enough to overcome every obstacle in your life. Your testimony gives you the strength to live for Him instead of living just for yourself.

I still remember how I celebrated on my way home after that experience as if it were yesterday. At the time, we were working through challenges in marriage, so I stopped in where my wife Lisa worked to tell her the good news. She laughed and then informed me that she had asked Christ into her heart at home the night before, and had asked God to get me. Wow; it is hard to outdo the wife!

When I got home I began to clean house. First the whiskey and beer went down the drain. Next the coke, crank and pounds of pot went into the burning barrel. All I had to light it with was white gas and when I tossed the match into the burning barrel it went two feet into the air accompanied by a loud explosion. Columns of burning pot smoke began to fill the air with the sweet smell of marijuana. The problem was that I lived on the north side of town and the wind was blowing south. To this day the people of Burlington, Pennsylvania don't know why they felt so good that day, but now the secret is out!

God has equipped us to be overcomers. But he leaves the choice to believe, live and draw upon the power of the scriptures with us. Remember, the blood cleanses us, our testimony equips us and love takes our eyes off of ourselves and onto a hurting humanity that needs to hear the powerful stories of our testimonies.

The Magnificent Seven

Made in the USA
Columbia, SC
01 November 2017